First published 28th of February 2023
Published in the UK by
Fly on the Wall Press
56 High Lea Rd
New Mills
Derbyshire
SK22 3DP

www.flyonthewallpress.co.uk
ISBN: 9781913211981

Copyright Viv Fogel © 2023

The right of Viv Fogel to be identified as the author of this work has been asserted in accordance with the Copyright, Designs and Patents Act 1988.
Typesetting by Isabelle Kenyon. Cover photo- Shutterstock and illustration author's own. Photo on page 30 by Anne Lambeck. All rights reserved. No part of this publication may be reproduced, stored in or introduced into a retrieval system, or transmitted in any form, or by any means (electronic, mechanical, photocopying, recording or otherwise) without prior written permissions of the publisher. Any person who does any unauthorised act in relation to this publication may be liable for criminal prosecution and civil claims for damages.

A CIP Catalogue record for this book is available from the British Library.

For Ralph (1946-2020)

and all those on their journey Home.

Contents

I

Exiled	9
Ahmad's Pool	11
After	13
Coracle	14
Couple's Therapy: Laura and Tim	15
The Nursing Chair	17
The Switch	18
When Poverty is a Keep Out Sign	19

II

My Father Sold Cigarettes To The Nazis	23
Oradour-Sur-Glâne	25
In Memoriam	27
And I Cannot Walk Over You	31
On Not Writing the Holocaust	32

III

Mr Rockwell	35
Her Fear of Water	36
White	37
Practical UnEnglish	38
In the House of Babi Yaga	40
First Meeting	43

IV

Bloodstream	47
Broken	49
Notebook	50
Still Point	51
Waiting For Jacob	53
Two For Joy	54
Spectral	56
Afterprint	58
Blue Jug	59
The Reading	60
Funeral	61
What Remains (a conversation)	62

V

Dawn Breaks on Ballywalter	67
The 'L' Word: a Poem About Love	68
Suffolk Spice	70
Night Drive	71
The Move	72
& this	74
I am Home	76
How It Is	77

I

*"No matter how kind and welcoming they are, I will never quite belong—
I will always be other—an outsider"*

These are the words I hear repeated over and over
from those who have had to leave their homeland;
it was my parent's experience as refugees, and it was
mine, both as an adoptee and on meeting
my birth family.

Exiled

i.

For one precious moment
you were my whole world
safe   holding and mine—
then gone.

I was alone
no roots
no ground.

The landscape changed:
familiar smells   textures
vanished   the terrain
became hostile.

ii.

Torn from your homeland
you strain towards a dream
beyond your grasp

the fruits you reach for
are a mirage. The sand
slipslides away

now is the waiting game:
questions   papers returned
visas granted   or delayed.

In yellow rooms you wait.
You sit watching the clock
not daring to hope.

Stranger
I welcome you
rootless as I
to this bittersweet land.

Ahmad's Pool

The therapod prints embedded in rocks were hidden—
until now.
The library of Alexandria—is still submerged under the
ocean.

What lies beneath the surface
often remains   unreachable

> *His unpaid debts   his shame*
> *how he begged her to forgive*

The waterlogged man who staggers ashore
from a capsized dinghy

collapses   trembling   into the arms of a volunteer
his head drops onto her shoulder   she rubs his back

for a moment he is
in the arms of his mother.

> *Tearful. A loving father.*
> *How he packed his bag and left—*

the chalk and blood-streaked face in shock
hauled from concrete and twisted girders,

the clutch of civilians clawing dust
to uncover—a hand to clasp? things-as-they-were-before?

> *They found him hanging from a tree,*
> *his bag spilled open beneath him*

In halting English   Ahmad describes his life
as a stagnant pool where nothing lives or moves.

Each night   he stands in moonlight   watching it shimmer,
the way light shimmers   the way light becomes a dart of
silver

a movement   a silver fish! the next night there are more—
and his pool starts to breathe

Back home I line my home-made pond with garden soil:
it's the wrong sort—it muddies and clouds the water—

if I wait patiently   it will clear

Ahmad, not his real name, was one of the asylum seekers I worked with, separated from his family. He now works for a refugee centre in the north of England.

After

With tiny 'o' of mouth, the newborn
latches on, nuzzling its urgency
upon her as they lie
hidden and safe.

She imagines beaches   shells
story times. Waking, she finds
she is alone   damp with milk
and a ghost child's tears.

There is no afterbirth   no handover.
I sit beside her as she rocks
her loss   remembering my own
then in the moss of woodland
dusk—a purple dazzle of O
a cluster of wild violets.

For H, a loved client, now passed, who chose not to have a baby as she was the carrier of a rare genetic and terminal disease. According to Bion 'O' is the ultimate truth: transformation in O is attained only by the willed surrender of memory, desire, sense gratification and understanding—perhaps even a surrender or letting go of the ego itself.

Coracle

> *Guten Abend, gute Nacht, mit Roslein bedacht,*
> *Mit Någlein besteckt, schlupf unter die Deck . . .**

Her mother placed her in a basket, hidden under patchwork,
and pushed her, wide-eyed and trusting, upstream.

For one whole day she floated, till sedge reeds
caught her, and a pale white moon found her.

Years passed. The child grew familiar with streams,
undercurrents, she played hide and seek

among the reeds, caught fish, then let them go,
envied that they could slip away. At night

she floated back, downstream, beneath trees
that wept, remembering patchwork. Far away,

the mother's basketry became legend:
her coracles crafted to lull, braided with longing—

cradles she would not rock, lullabies she would not hum,
songs for a child forever drifting.

* *Good evening, good night, go to sleep covered*
with tiny roses, under a blanket of lilies . . .

(from Brahms Lullaby or Cradle Song)

Couple's Therapy: Laura and Tim*

He:
rises early before the light/sorts the day
while she still sleeps/tells himself
she's fine

She:
not fine/not asleep/dreads
the day ahead/fearful that this
fragile newness might break

she's surfing the edge/
dark waves of terror/baby's
uncertain breath

He:
smiles down his hurt/wipes away
his dreams/closes the door
shuts them out/embraces

the sun's outstretched arms:
it makes no sense
but work comforts him

She:
is back then   to that
slow-motion, numb-dull
s t r e t c h of hours

            w a i t i n g

'til he returns
needing her reassurance/
her brightly-applied smile

not their real names

The Nursing Chair

lay hidden under baize in the muddle
of the auction rooms, its cover faded, its rosewood arm
peeping out, and I knew then that it needed a home.

At first you did not see me, hidden in the corner
under utility beige, you walked right past
the huddle of cots—till my baby fingers waved

as if to stop you—and you knew then
that you would bring me home, because I needed you,
because of my small and beckoning fist.

Solemn eyes under dark brows, your wiry hair pinned back,
a smell I did not belong to: how could you hold or comfort
when you yourself were exiled and broken?

The chair sits low on the ground, its back straight, a nursing chair
that has midwifed mothers, some eager, some numbed,
others dreaming themselves into another place, another life.

Decades on, the chair listens, solid and soothing,
its seat stained with ink, pawed and clawed by the cats.
It creaks, warmed with laughter, stitches gape, the fluff

and stuffing escapes like a grey frizzed perm,
and bits bulge where they should not.
I pat tenderly, promising to fix it—soon.

The Switch

O cuckoo—you usurper you—such trickery!
Such deceit! To filch, takeover another's nest,
throw out the other's eggs before they hatch,
disguise your own—with perfect colour-match.
Such artistry, such cunning and skill,
to ensure a home—protect then leave.

Does the nesting songbird sense the switch,
smell out her changeling egg? Will she host
yet punish it for this maternal heist?

Cuckoo's first call is heard on April 14th,
my birth date. Taken to another's nest,
with name and feathers I could not keep,
I became the strange one who did not fit.

O cuck-mother—do you not miss your own?

When Poverty is a Keep Out Sign

and shame the smell that follows you,
when you wear your school shirt inside out,
to hide the frayed and unwashed collar,

when there's a whiff of menstruation
you hope goes unnoticed, like the
sock stained at the toe that sticks,

and opens the wound when pulled,
when you keep your eyes downcast
for fear they will be met

where d'you go child?

•

I see you
all slouch and kick-kerb,
in tight-scuffed trainers,

you glitter-search garbage,
rummage-sift store-bins, niff
of sell-bys, your hunger growling

When there's no place to chill,
the centre's closed, and the park
lurks with winos and dealers

where's there to go?

•

Some get wasted in piss-foul alleys
swagger their tales   score'n dare
compare blades   suck-teeth

as you pass by   in worn out
hood tight breath eyes down
        silently praying
        to stay invisible

II

*When your children ask you why—
what will you reply?*

*And where does light hide
when the world is in darkness?*

From *Six Questions in Search of an Answer* - Viv Fogel

My Father Sold Cigarettes To The Nazis
for Itzaak Weinreich b.1903 - d.1988

blue-eyed and handsome, he nodded and grinned
at them through the coffee houses of Berlin, the cakes
and cabaret, a sweet tooth and an eye for women.

He wrote funny verse, made his friends laugh,
turned horror into humour, played the joker,
protected me from the truth.

My father loved to polish: wooden banisters,
brass door handles, candlesticks—our boots;
always polishing.

Buchenwald was his camp: *'but Butlins it was not!'*
I wasn't meant to hear about the officer's
leather belt, his polished boots,

of the baby tossed
into the air, skull
cracking beneath the boot.

And once, he upturned the kitchen table,
mouth foaming, as plates slid
cracking to the floor.

He died a year before the Wall came down,
the year my baby was born.
I sat by his bed and fed *him*,

as once he fed me. I stroked his baby head,
made him smile at *my* jokes,
as his watery eyes were fading.

I traced his burnt-scarred arm, tapped
my fingers along numbers the same blue-grey
as his veins, longing to unlock his story.

He held my baby in his arms, just once,
a little awkward, a little shy,
a big man   grown small.

Oradour-Sur-Glâne

It's teatime in Oradour. You can smell the apple flan
baked by Gran'mémé   red cheeked at the hot oven
wiping her floury arms; you can see the smeared lipstick
of a flustered wife in her polka dot frock
wiping away a kiss   hurrying
back to her children
who wait for her.

It's teatime in Oradour. The soldiers entered.
In the meadow behind the barn they took the men and boys.
The church was locked: inside women screaming,
the children muffled by the roaring falling timber.
That red hot afternoon in June, at 16h 31,
the hands on all the clocks and watches
stopped.

In the concrete grey and glass it's the red I notice:
resin comb, button, the peeling paint of a toy truck,
a child's scuffed shoe. Then the rosebud lips of a doll,
hair singed, eyes glassy, wide, and then the markings
in a child's book and a tin box with its ledger of receipts.
And there's a charred scrap of red polka dots on white.

At the blackened altar below the stained window:
pram wheels, push chairs.
It didn't take long.

Picking a small red apple from the ground
I smell the tarte aux pommes.
It's teatime in Oradour.

On June 10th 1944, in reprisal to French resistance, German soldiers marched into Oradour-sur-Glane and set fire to the village, murdering its residents.

In Memoriam

For my mother Henriette, her brother Karl, the uncle I never met, and for their parents Mechel and Yette, the grandparents I never knew, shot in the pine forests of Maly Trostinec, Belarus.

1   Mother

Memories stalk   from room to room
        saucepans   boiling bones
kettle screams   shower steams   smell of fear
guilt-furred tongue names faces   she recalls
                                     side-steps
broken glass   night terrors
                       whimpering   raging
numbers on her arm
                turned raw with picking

2   Uncle (d.1939 aged 27)

As the soldiers advanced
her 'baby' brother
(blue-eyes/blonde-curls/cravat/
keyboard-fingers/nightclub-jazz)
knew what he had to do—

                       she wept for him
and buried him with the family's sorrow.

3   Grandparents

Zayde's neat and even script:
> *The sun light dazzling through the trees*
> *oh! there's a vivid blue butterfly!*
> *— we're still waiting for our visas*

the paper he wrote on   tissue thin   fragile
> *work hard   be polite   keep your head down*
> *— we will soon be together —*

4

> Sun light in a forest—
> and a blue butterfly

Memorial installation 'Shalekhet': Fallen Leaves at the Jewish Museum in Berlin 2014

And I Cannot Walk Over You

Fallen leaves do not clink like this
beneath your feet   but these leaves
clank like steel plates in a breaker's yard
chattels and goods broken down beneath
you   the continuous clatter punctuated
by faint chimes   cries   *shalekhet*.

There are other holocausts
other stories   other memories
but this   this is what I know
is what I came from
and for you my body re-
members.

Fallen leaves are russet
crisp underfoot. But you
you melt slowly   your
bones   blacken   calcify
your   mouths gasp
shafts of gaseous light.

On Not Writing the Holocaust

I was not there—yet when I see
dense forests, barbed wire, rail-tracks,
something in me remembers—

the stench of it slips between the lines
urges me to transcribe, make sense of it
but I can't—I was not there

striped pyjamas, a soft leather valise,
a postcard from the Stoke Potteries
funnels of dark smoke unfurling

a lost child's shoe by the canal
the absence of birdsong
a field of stones and silence

many will roll their eyes   *Move on*
so I do not write about the Holocaust
I was not there   I was not there

III

I am the daughter of darkness:
dancing on the graves of our fathers,
spilling my sacred blood,
demanding sacrifice.

Will you accept my grief?

From *Melancholia* - Viv Fogel

Mr Rockwell

There are no photos but I imagine you sucking on a cigar,
your stubby nails manicured, a gold diamond ring maybe.

I found the faded list of things you paid for: bonnet and bootees,
a knitted coat, a blanket for the cot, formula milk, adoption fees.

My bewildered mother was made to leave, her breasts full
and aching, and a new home was found for me.

They told me you were fat—a wandering
hand that patted, groped and squeezed—

but you were their boss and the girls were malleable.
No expectations you told them so nothing lost!

Your accent thick as the lies you told your wife.
Years later I track you down, call your home.

A curt voice informs me that you're dead.
Click—the contact is cut. But Father,

I need your eyes, your smell, your look—
to see how akin the echo

Her Fear of Water

In the cyclone of lost years that spiral down she is caught by an abrupt shift of mood a flash a glint a subtle turn warm then cold unpredictable like a freak storm at sea. She rides the waves a child cradled with ambivalence rocked by virgin blue where terror lurks in the downward pull of pre-verbal-fear to the almost-death/ in the letting down/and the letting go/ she eases her breath/at last/allowing the Darkness to carry her

White

The room is white   whiter than the lies she fed you
when her taunts stuck in your throat   like the food
forced down you   nostrils pinched/ *open your mouth/*
one orifice stuffed   the other purged with an enema
for your own good, she spat, *to rid you of the evil*
she swore you came from

when the beatings with the wooden butter-pat
left red welts across your calves
when the tangle of hair pulled tight
was a scalping   when the woollen
vests she made you wear itched

like the straitjacket they made her wear
for her own good   after the white pills
after the white coats watched warily
after they moved her into that white room.

Practical UnEnglish

Mutti claimed the Nazis butchered her so she couldn't have babies:
I believed her. But she should never have taken me instead.
Guilt-sick, she could not keep me safe. She force-fed,

fattened me, straightened my hair with tongs, tugged at
my thick-tangled curls, twisted them tightly into plaits pulled
Gretchen-like around my head until, in spite, despite

my pleas, she made me cut it short. She drew in my liberty
bodice—until I could hardly breathe, trampled my singular
joys, my confidence, told me I was ugly.

No child of mine, she hissed—with venom in her eyes.
No child of yours, I'd think, consoling myself.
Her pain became my art and then my craft. And yet

she loved: Goethe's Erlkönig, Shubert's Lieder, Tauber,
the piano she made me sing to, in pink taffeta, for guests.
She sewed clothes for me, a coat even, practical, un-English.

The garden she created shone with colour. We visited Kew,
she showed me beauty and poetry in nature, and the tower
where Rapunzel remained trapped. How I longed to free her.

Her strong accent shamed me, her haunted awkwardness.
The stories she told became unbearable, seeped
with tears for those who perished, those she left behind.

She swallowed handfuls of pills in front of me,
so they sent me away, gave her ECT. And yet
she baked, her Powidltascherl and Apfelstrüdel were divine.

Dying, she blamed Vati and I both. She blamed
the Nazis. She blamed   turned her naked, scarfed head
to the wall, eyes dulled with disappointment,

her body swollen and spongey, the sweat
and bulk of her: stranded   gasping her last
on bleak English shingle.

In the House of Babi Yaga

She never asked to be brought here to this house perched on the edge
of the valley. Outside, a menacing poplar blocks the sun. Inside, the walls
are beige with bamboo, floral carpets swirl, the divan is olive green, G-Plan.

She remembers her soiled pants on the wooden draining board, the butter-pat
that left red welts across her calves. Her mother's sickness a storm
that ripped open the dawn curtains ordering her to dust and polish.

Envy called her ugly, pulled tight her tangled hair.
Mistrust screamed on the midnight doorstep, calling her liar and slut.

She pockets her voice beside her small rag-doll Vassilisa, swallows
her secrets like forbidden sweets, imagines a palace under the sea,
and draws comfort from the patterns of waves and shells.

She's a princess   waiting   for the spell
to be broken.

My mother's grief was a hunger, eating away at her, an envious laugh, a vicious rasp, a sound that spat at us and turned itself against the world. We lived in the shadow of her discontent—no— her profound self-hatred. My father died not knowing he was loved for she could not even love herself. Older now than she ever became, it's taken me a lifetime to release her shame.

*I contemplate the comfort of sewing / the rejoining of things torn apart
and how after the repair / the threads are tied and cut.*

From *Threads* - Viv Fogel

First Meeting
For my birth mother, Jennie

Unconscious in a hospital bed,
she grips my finger, as one tear
from the corner of her eye rolls down
when I whisper who I am.

I've made good my life, I say
and comatose she responds:
one squeeze for yes, two for no.
I hold onto her hand.

I had imagined this moment
seen her draw back   hesitate to rejoin
what she was made to sever
both of us wavering.

*

I meet her friends, her sister—and her son
(WOW—a half-brother!) who tell me
how alike our gestures, our goofy teeth.

I tell her about Jo, her grand-daughter—and
'I look forward to seeing more of you'. A squeeze.
'No blame, no regrets'—and, 'I love staying in your flat.'

The cartoons tacked inside her kitchen cupboards
remind me of mine; I am proud of her hidden awards
(for services to the community) those shields, those plaques,
tucked out of sight, swaddled in soft towels.

*

On this no-one-else-but-us shore,
this then becomes our beginning.
The space between   hovers   liminal—
there are no memories to replace what was lost,
yet, emptiness longs to be filled with what it once knew—
isn't that enough?

IV

"Only when you suffer the pangs and tribulations of exile will you truly enjoy your homecoming."
- Rumi

"Your homecoming will be my homecoming."
- e.e.cummings

Bloodstream

1

My daughter rages
she sides
with the underdog   hates
what she cannot fix
her eagle eye   watchful
ready to swoop   to kill
anger keeps her   alive

When she was small
I was lonely   and sad
too tired to mother   pushed
her   away
paid for that—
        (and therapy)
so she could   hate me
       and   she did

2

a dark panther of   fury
propelled me   across the room
knocked my head   against a wall
blamed and   shook
me in its teeth

           at night she'd creep
             into my bed
              and weep

most days she was bright-eyed
her stand-up   gestures
mime   songs & dances
funny faces
made us laugh   still do

Broken
For Jo

Funny philosophical mimic
your teenage jokes tease
as we dance sisterly and rude

but last year's shame
stole your smile   walled
your face to stone

your lids weighted with lies
your sorrowful shoulders
I watch from a distance

as you switch off your light

Notebook

My daughter enjoys the safety of lines,
but I prefer the blank page, to dive

and spiral bird free in a cloudless sky.
She cuts paper into delicate shapes,

pastes petals, turns butterflies into collages,
begins again if there is one mistake.

I splatter words like Pollock onto clear canvas
and smudge, rub holes in paper, stain and tear.

My daughter bathes in milk, soaks in Caribb sun,
paints her nails as bright as her imagined future.

She perfects her dress, her look, takes t i m e,
whereas I, careless, will wear the same for days.

She emerges at last, silky in a swirl
of turquoise, pink ipod, humming out of tune,

as I wait for her in the afternoon's heat,
my hand's shadow on the filling page.

Still Point
"to call myself beloved, to feel myself beloved on the earth"
- Raymond Carver: Late Fragment

We face each other - drawing back.
Does it matter which one goes first?

The house breathes. Your bed's unmade
your toothbrush gone. Books, hairbands,

blu-tac marks, a dream-board of plans, graffitti on the door,
its panels felt-marked with a love-ladder of friends,

promises: READ, be nice to mum, DON'T bite nails,
help wash up, eat sensibly, DON"T tell lies.

Your grey-green eyes scan mine for approval.

*

In the care-unit a woman breathes into her life.

And an incubate newborn also breathes—fingers
curled around his mother's gloved thumb.

Does it matter how imperfect the beginning?
how flawed the end?

we improvise
singing to songs we've never heard.

What I know Jo, is that still point
in moving water

and after all the blame and hurt,
you and I can still laugh and joke.

What I know is when we dance
the ground holds us   both   beloved.

Waiting For Jacob

Long before you come we prepare speak your name
marvel how in utero you suck your thumb,
blow bubbles—your long legs and feet restless
kicking—a footballer like your dad. This time
we say, after so many losses it'll be alright—
and so we sing for you

My daughter lets me watch   be with her.
I cool her beaded body with a cloth,
remind her to breathe   to will your safety
and through the waves of pain   she cries
and laughs delirious for gas and air.

When you finally push through
blood crowning   slimed wet and blue
wrapped and weighed too early too soon
we hold our breath then drop with relief
that you have—against all odds—arrived.

Two For Joy
For Jacob 4.5 and Thea almost 3

I'm climbing to the sky Nonna   catch me
squeal-of-delight   face bright
                              oh! there's my shadow
                              and that's my echo when I scream
              an' mine! shouts number-two-who's-almost-three

so hop jump 'n tumble
                    clamber   scrumble
                                        on fallen trunk
to flake off bark: watch insects scuttle off to hide
queen and king of castle
                        whee!!
                                          and break-off-
branch
wave magic wand/super-sword
                            twigs to throw and water-skim
just missing geese

Look Nonna   how far I throwed! 'Well done,' I say, *I win!* says he
            an' me! cries number-two-who's-almost-three

'See the swans?' I point—'no not allowed to feed'—
Why not?
'and look—see the magpies? Two for joy   three for…?'

Daisies! she claps—*can we make a chain?* and dandelions—
'Do you need to wee? okay don't scream—you'll scare those dogs!
or chase the pigeons or stamp-the-ants'—*but they're small!*
'Yes—but busy in their lives not hurting anyone—'

Oh look a bee—is he asleep? and a slug—yuk!

Nonna—what's this? what's that?

         jump-off   land-crunch in
dust-dry-leaves
         or hop-splash   puddle-happy
                                           splatter-grin

NOT an ice-cream Nonna a lolly please!
                      cries number-two-who's-almost-three

The sun is burning my eyes
              oh see—there's a real strawberry inside!

Just one more ride see-saw slide—do we have to go home now?

Sun cools   empty   playground
    pink-clouds   sky-pond
                       head lolls (she-who's-almost-three)
with snuffle-breath and buggy-snore

                    he trots beside with
magic-stick
      all quiet now
                   and
                         home

Spectral
For Jacob

the corner of his room / is goose-bump cold/ SHE strokes to wake him /
eyes-wide / he sits up / still-asleep / as she whispers a mother's loss / certain
she'll not be heard / I hear / soothe her / no need to stay / it's safe to leave /
the room clears / he sleeps on / dreams other voices / calling / calling / he wakes /

drenched with FURY / his ancestors / their revenge / THUMPS his sister / screeches /
I try to restrain him: WON'T / held down / enslaved / chains / fight back / break free /
WHO SPEAKS? / yet I know / I AM his past / and mine / red-eyes / spike / his skinny-brown / child's body /
quivering / **branded** / searing / taking me back—

and I am five / a family Easter-Pesach / new television-set / HORRIFIED/ as black and white Christ /
is nailed to the cross / the Last Agony / each nail / driven / Uncle Max carries me / thrashing /
SCREAMING/ feverish / to another room / calm down CALM DOWN!

SHE / ghost-mother is back / incomprehension / at my daughter's pregnancy /
to carry our babes / to lose them / WHY? / new arrivals / silent shuffle / mothers / children / sifted / to the left / if fit / to the right / if sick / *lie about you age / what you can do /*

OR / crated / white-tight grip / under lorry / or crammed / on boats / foil-wrapped /
shivering / I know them / those children / at the borders / caged / parentless /
WHO / speaks for them? / my brown grandson / rocks himself / not knowing /
that he re-members / that he is part of / that we are all part of

he twists / hears whispers / a spectrum of voices / he does not understand /
his rage / shocks him / he has pummelled / the swollen belly / of his mother /
her blondness / her white skin / WHO ARE YOU? / You are / NOT / my mum

FURIOUS / as I felt-tip / his afro-curls black / insists that Black is Bad / and yells
DON'T / colour me brown / WHO TAUGHT HIM THIS? / just as /
she-who-was-not-my-birthmother / hissed / unseeing in her madness /
WHO are you? / You are not mine / I lost my daughter—

a drift of voices / the spectres' keening / mangled memories / dredged / from the ocean bed /
the stench / filth and foulness / of our pasts / dark echoes that vibrate / along the timelines /
strings / of a cello / in the courtyard / played to survive /
listen   / we hear you

Afterprint

this wristwatch has left its mark—a pale
luscent disc like the flattened wheat of
a crop circle   balding what's absent
on my tanned wrist naked as the day
we come in   blanched as the
moment we must leave: an everyday
reminder of how small and separate
we are as time leaves its afterprint

Blue Jug

When they first told her, she went up to her neglected studio
pulled out an unused canvas and prepared to paint. Squeezed

the ceruleum blue and let it roll, as if a wave of deep warm sea, then
bolder strokes of yellow chrome to bring in the long forgotten sun.

The magentas, violets and oranges she kept
until last: the colours of her past.

They live in separate houses. His is filled with trophies,
hers is filled with colour. He reads, she paints.

She bakes a lemon-yellow cake and places it on Tuscan green.
Colours take on an intensity and the garden glows.

In the fading light a scent of roses and jasmine,
and the orange-purple sky is another canvas.

She is dying. And he is afraid of his fear.
He reads, she paints.

One by one she invites her beloveds
and thanks them. And him, especially him.

She is patting objects, letting them go.
She sees the blue jug, with its carefully

glued crack, takes it down and uses it
for the very first time.

The Reading
For E

In the Owl Bookshop a dark eyed woman
with silver hair reads her poems, whilst we
smile, murmur, exchange looks: we know
this launch is both a debut and a finale.

She remembers: her roots, her stepmother,
her grandparents; she remembers landscapes,
textures, the smells and sounds of her childhood.
Her daughters and her friends read for her,

as her words are passed on, retold with care.
The woman shimmers, fatigued. We notice
her frail wrist, breathless voice. She signs
her name, whispers that the chemo's done.

This *is* the memoriam. There are triangles
of thin bread, fishballs. Wine glasses
are filled, as we move towards
each other   as she turns away.

Funeral

From parked cars come the bent and the bowed,
the frail step cautiously in ill prepared shoes.

Tenderness shelters under a huddle of umbrellas,
the mourners disperse like sad patches on a lawn.

The lawn is slabbed to make room for the coffin.
The coffin tilts like a half-smile and when I shovel

earth onto it   clods of guilt   land with a thump.
My guilt goes unnoticed   travels hooded like an illegal

immigrant crossing the border   immigrants learn to play
their instruments in silence—which is like an orchestra

without sound—which is what it must be like just before
you slip over to the other side.

What Remains (a conversation)

The leaving and the return:
in the tool-shed, four baby swallows
ready to fledge: their parents teach them
how to feed; prepare them for the six thousand miles
        and each year they find their way back
      same location same shed—and a few won't
the leaving and the return
as the tide comes and goes
the breathing in the breathing out

a dog frisks the edge of the waves *I want to be ordinary nothing more*
a quad bike makes tracks motor purring
          I just don't want to die
a silver-haired couple jog past the heat of sun
on thigh damp toes repeated *sssshhhh* of the sea
        I wonder which of us will go first?
Two wetsuits drying on the upturned kayak.
Those prints etchings sculptures of found beach-objects
do not compare to this

      maybe just being in beauty is enough?

Two exotic palms landmark the grounds
pampas grasses fringe the path
the plank quivers slips to the beach. Worm coils bouclé
the wet sand its rock-pools nippled limpets
one dulled plastic bottle lodged in the mulch of seaweed

      good for compost— not supposed to bag it but—

the newly-seeded lawns flower beds
greenhouses   vegetable plots   orchards

                         a never-ending task we'll just leave behind
the sea-green writing cabin binoculars:
                    on a clear day you can see the Isle of Man
a committee of terns on the whale-hump rocks
                      look—when the night skies are aflame
                        see how they illuminate the clouds?
the leaving   and the return
two small white boats

                  moored   and   waiting.

V

remembering
what's been
forgotten

from *Night Drive* (P.71)

The art of re-membering for me is a coming back to that which once belonged, that may have been cut off from us—or dis-membered. In our busy, defended and urban lives, we are often complicit in this—separating our selves, our bodies and our hearts from what sustains and nourishes us … For me, nature restores and I need to honour and re-member her.

Dawn Breaks on Ballywalter

and a silvery gold laces the sky. Gulls swoop and the terns
chatter noisily. A heron perches on a distant rock.

Around the lichen-covered Whale's Back, rivulets swirl
and worm coils pattern the damp mud between my feet.

Back home time squeezes itself like the last insufficient drop
onto a sink full of leftovers. Here time is slow and s p a c i o u s.

Wild grasses stretch like dancers towards the water
and a pair of cabbage whites hover above the ferns.

A speckled sky spreads itself across the glittering horizon.
The dawn is pierced by the mournful cries of curlews

repeating themselves. Words cut their truth like new teeth:
sometimes there is such beauty that it hurts.

The 'L' Word: a Poem About Love

"You'll do," you said, forty years after
we'd first met and the tributary of our lives
had parted, only to return once more
from the lives we'd lived with others,
with other rituals, other endurances.

I questioned 'Love'—but my heart persisted,
as when painting the hall-way, roller in hand,
you reached over precariously balancing
under the skylight—and we laughed.
Look my heart nudged can't you see
when it's in front of you?

I see you tutoring my daughter maths,
catching my eye, then hers;
or lost inside your head nodding
to the 'download' of a symphony.

You choose and compile music for me,
plant tulip bulbs and daffodils,
encourage me on cycle rides, inform me
about the neighbourhood, its history,
the trees, the changing landscape;
you arrive with home-cooked casseroles,
"meals on wheels," you grin—

So now I'm in it for the long haul—
because despite your missing teeth,
your smile still dazzles and despite
your acquired vernacular,
that hides your background and class,

and your couldn't-care-less frayed collars,
and the torn elbows of beloved shirts,
and the chalk'n cheese of us, we dance well
together and our bodies fit, delighting us still

so that when you turn away from me,
my back misses the curled cradle of you,
and I am grateful that we are here now,
for whatever time allows us,
to have and to hold whatever this is:

this Love   that is not just a feeling,
this Love   that speaks not in words,
this Love   that is a verb.

Annie Lawson Illustration

Suffolk Spice

The cottage hides on the edge of fields,
its fire-damaged thatch retiled now. The grass
a yellow-bald patch where the skip had been.

Bridal blossom and piercing periwinkle
quiver beneath the newly-painted sill.

In a corner of the old laundry-shed
a peacock butterfly hibernates
and sleeping ladybirds cluster.

The twisted apple tree stoops
over an emptied wheelbarrow.

We trudge towards the swell of river
past flood-swamped fields of sedge
the high-pitched trill of reed warblers.

Across a sky shredded purple and pink
the sun lowers itself into night

You run a bath   I light candles
shadows flickerdance on limewashed
stone to the harmonium of King Creosote

flames spit   crackle   a whiff of wood-burn.
Venus gleams lustrous in ink-dark velvet.

Night Drive

An absence of mothwing
against the windscreen
no startled deer, owl hoot
or nightingales:
we sit   separated
in thought
past roadkill
plastic-sheeted fields
shimmer like lakes.

The motorway
stretches before us
a fleet of army trucks
tarp-covered tanks
rumbles past
your hands
grip the wheel.

Suddenly
from behind
the shadowed hump
of trees we see the full
Pink Moon: orange
in the darkening sky

we hold
           our breath
remembering
what's been
forgotten.

The Move

and suddenly the air seems sweeter,
stillness smiles slow-motion from a distance,
the birdsong is clear, confident,
and in my new street strangers pass
and nod, as if to say stay safe, take care.

In warm April sun Alan planes and putties,
blades open paint-encrusted frames: windows
ancient, locked, uneven flaking sills.
He chops wood, makes shelves, clears
the rubbled ivy of garden. We clean,
sort, open boxes, catch each other's eyes,
realising with relief how blessed we are,
how in time, how graced in our cocoon.

The grandkids WhatsApp, show their drawings,
sing a song just learnt, report the day—
his scratch, her fall; we choose the bedtime story,
they kiss the screen, hug the phone,
butterfly kisses are blown.

In last night's dream I wrapped a cloak
around our blue and gasping planet,
a net of light to help it breathe,
blew away dust-clouds of viral fear,
hosed clean the darkened rivers.

Next morning   outside our bedroom window,
the magnolia is in second bloom,
pale pink   pure   perfect.

We moved in together a week before the first lockdown in March 2020—a week later and it would have all fallen through.

& this

i   tallit

each morning I enter you like a tent:
peace welcomes me
heart stirs together
we welcome the day.

ii   this

in this emptiness
a richness
in this space
no-thing
time suspended

floats
is soft   silent.

in this silence
your heartbeat
breath gentle slows
body containing knows

heart opens
into love
simple and pure

there is
nothing
more
than
this

iii   opening

next to my skin
at the place
of bone and heart
I have made an opening
for you to enter

silently
my bone life
remembers

next to my heart
where breath
softens you slip in
welcomed
at last

touching darkness
we meet

Tallit: a Jewish prayer-shawl

I am Home
Chania Old Town, Crete

The synagogue of Etz Hayyim once vandalised
and left in ruins is renovated now

its star-gated courtyard a sanctuary:
olive tree   shade   stillness

The brass sign reads:
All faiths and everyone welcome here.

Tombstone fragments   slow heat of afternoon
orange blossoms sweeten the air

Beyond the walled arch   a glimpse
of harbour and Cretan blue

Lilac-misted mountains surround
and hold me

In Arabic Hani means joy
in Hebrew Hania is peace.

How It Is

1

I don't want clever
I want simple and true
words that take me to the raw

What is there to fear?
why return again
to what stops you?

Smell the earth after rain
the air is velvet as it breathes
the sodden ground still holds

One child is born
another dies
no reason   this is how it is.

2

Light shafts through a gap
in the blinds as I peel myself
from the fit of your body

The cat nudges
purring her request
against my leg

I savour my green tea
scent of hyacinths on the sill
full emptiness of sky

In this still moment
the first snowdrop
stretches towards the sun

Acknowledgements and Thanks

Many thanks to the editors of the following publications in which some of these poems, or earlier versions of, have appeared.
Artemis, (Second Light); *Morton Press; New Gallery Books; Writes of Women: Haringey Libraries & Arts* (Arts Council funded); *Pluto Press; Mandaras; Homebound Poetry; Fly on the Wall* (Demos Rising)

Oradour-sur-Glâne was highly commended in a Second Light Poetry Competition.

I wish I could say I entered competitions or won prizes and awards—but I don't—unless pushed (like for the above) —but a big thanks to those that do push me: Jacqueline Saphra for her spot on critique, inspirational group tutoring (Crouch End Poets) and individual mentoring, her humanity and activism; Julian Bishop for his gentle presence, recognition and support, and for directing me towards Fly on the Wall—despite our very different writing styles; thanks to all those, past and present, in my Palmers Green stanza group and in the Crouch End Poets—(too numerous to name—they know who they are), and Annie Lawson for her delightful cartoon and her Homebound Poetry pamphlets of mine; Dr. Jennifer Langer and Catherine Davidson et al at EWI (Exile Writers Ink) for all that EWI does to encourage writers to heal from this bruised and fragile world of exiles.

Through it all—where would I be without my family and friends, (another family)—so big appreciation to my old friends who are constants in my life: Mick for being my soul-brother; Lesley for her listening time, understanding and sisterhood, and all the wonderful women who inspire me in our OWLs (older women local support) group.

I thank too the profoundly courageous and inspiring people I work with, whose stories I am privileged to hear, whose dreams and hopes I witness.

A big thank you also to Isabelle Kenyon, for her endless patience and belief in my work; her encouraging words when I doubted, and for supporting me through this project. I wish I'd listened to her 'orange' choice of cover!

Finally for Jo and the kids, and for my partner Alan, who show me how to love, belong, and be part of a family—hard though that is. I am still learning. I thank you.

For more information on my experience and legacy of adoption I have a chapter in the book Chosen: Living with Adoption (edited by Perlita Harris) - published in 2012 by BAAF (British Association of Adoption & Fostering) which is used as a text book for Social Work students.

Author Biography

Viv Fogel was born in Kent in 1948 and adopted ten months later by two refugee Holocaust survivors who escaped from the Nazis and met in this country. Her adoptive mother was bi-polar (or manic-depressive as it was then called) and Viv learnt to self soothe with drawing and poetry and, much later, therapy.

As an Islington based artist and art teacher, she was involved with adult and community education projects, mural painting and the mid-70's licensed squatting movement which provided free studio space.

Her first poem was published in Peace News when she was sixteen. Since then, her poetry has been published in various magazines and anthologies and heard on radio. In the early 80's she was part of a performing quartet of feminist poets called the Evettes and in the 90's she co-organised local poetry and music events.

Her first collection was Without Question in 2006 and she has two pamphlets: Witness (2013) and How it is (2018).

Viv has worked as a psychotherapist for almost 40 years, a supervisor for 30 years and, since 2011, as a mentor and trainer for those who incorporate energy-psychotherapy into their practices. She gives talks, works internationally, writes about her work (a vocation) and is trying to 'do less' gracefully. She lives with her partner and an orange cat, not far from her daughter and three grandchildren.

www.vivfogel.co.uk

About Fly on the Wall Press

A publisher with a conscience.
Political, Sustainable, Ethical.
Publishing politically-engaged, international fiction, poetry and cross-genre anthologies on pressing issues. Founded in 2018 by founding editor, Isabelle Kenyon.

Some other publications:

The Woman With An Owl Tattoo by Anne Walsh Donnelly
The Prettyboys of Gangster Town by Martin Grey
The Sound of the Earth Singing to Herself by Ricky Ray
Medusa Retold by Sarah Wallis
Pigskin by David Hartley
We Are All Somebody
Aftereffects by Jiye Lee
Someone Is Missing Me by Tina Tamsho-Thomas
Odd as F*ck by Anne Walsh Donnelly
Muscle and Mouth by Louise Finnigan
Modern Medicine by Lucy Hurst
These Mothers of Gods by Rachel Bower
Sin Is Due To Open In A Room Above Kitty's by Morag Anderson
Fauna by David Hartley
How To Bring Him Back by Clare HM
Hassan's Zoo and A Village in Winter by Ruth Brandt
No One Has Any Intention of Building A Wall by Ruth Brandt
Snapshots of the Apocalypse by Katy Wimhurst
Demos Rising
Exposition Ladies by Helen Bowie
A Dedication to Drowning by Maeve McKenna
We Saw It All Happen by Julian Bishop

Social Media:

@fly_press (Twitter) @flyonthewallpress (Instagram)

@flyonthewallpress (Facebook)

www.flyonthewallpress.co.uk